WHAT I FEEL

I AM WORRIED

Beth Gottlieb

first concepts

Gareth Stevens
PUBLISHING

I am worried.

I start school today.
I am worried.

I meet Ms. Penn.
She helps me!

I have a dance show.
I am worried.

I tell my dad.
We take deep breaths.
I am ready to dance!

I am getting a shot.

I am worried.

The nurse tells me

I am brave!

I see a bee.
I do not want a
bee sting.
I am worried!

The bee goes
to a flower.
I walk away.
I feel better.

There are lots of people at the party. I am worried.

I tell a friend.
He says it is OK
to feel worried.
He stays with me.

Everyone feels worried sometimes. What makes you feel worried?

Please visit our website, www.garethstevens.com. For a free color catalog of all our high-quality books, call toll free 1-800-542-2595 or fax 1-877-542-2596.

Library of Congress Cataloging-in-Publication Data

Names: Gottlieb, Beth author
Title: I am worried / Beth Gottlieb.
Description: [Buffalo] : Gareth Stevens Publishing, [2027] | Series: What I feel
Identifiers: LCCN 2025027273 (print) | LCCN 2025027274 (ebook) | ISBN 9781482476156 (library binding) | ISBN 9781482476149 (paperback) | ISBN 9781482476163 (ebook)
Subjects: LCSH: Worry in children–Juvenile literature | Worry–Juvenile literature | Emotions in children–Juvenile literature | LCGFT: Literature
Classification: LCC BF723.W67 G67 2027 (print) | LCC BF723.W67 (ebook) | DDC 155.4/1246–dc23/eng/20250818
LC record available at https://lccn.loc.gov/2025027273
LC ebook record available at https://lccn.loc.gov/2025027274

Published in 2027 by
Gareth Stevens Publishing
2544 Clinton Street
Buffalo, NY 14224

Designer: Deanna Lepovich
Editor: Therese Shea

Photo credits: Cover Tartila/Shutterstock.com; cover, pp. 3, 5, 7, 9, 11, 13, 15, 17, 19, 21, 23 (texture) v_kulieva/Shutterstock.com; p. 3 Krakenimages.com/Shutterstock.com; p. 5 Iam_Anuphone/Shutterstock.com; p. 7 PeopleImages/Shutterstock.com; pp. 9, 11 CREATISTA/Shutterstock.com; p. 13 Gorodenkoff/Shutterstock.com; p. 15 Yuliya Evstratenko/Shutterstock.com; p. 17 tiffanychipman/Shutterstock.com; p. 19 Ground Picture/Shutterstock.com; p. 21 Khorzhevska/Shutterstock.com; p. 23 GOLFX/Shutterstock.com.

Printed in China

CPSIA compliance information: Batch #QSGS27: For further information contact Gareth Stevens at 1-800-542-2595.